Human Resource Management

Author: Amy Sculler

H R MANAGEMENT

Table of Contents

UNIT 1
INTRODUCTION TO HUMAN RESOURCE MANAGEMENT

There are several categories that make up an entire organization. Employees in an organization are specifically hired to provide and/or facilitate the daily operations of the business. Even the labor provided by an employee is a resource, but it will now be called human resource. The human resource in a business is sectioned under the Human Resource management.

What is Human Resource Management?

Also referred to as HRM, this is the process of recruiting, and evolving employees, in order for them to become more productive for the given organization. The HRM can also be described as a function that deals with the recruitment and management of the employees in an organization. HR management can also be responsible for the provision of guidelines for the employees. There could be specific human resource managers, but in some organizations, the owner or a delegate would be responsible.

Principles Of HRM

This is a complex unit that needs to be followed and handled critically. There are some values that are usually laid down in most organizations, which functions as a blueprint. Here are the top principles of HRM:

1. Commitment

Every organization needs each employee to show commitment in their assigned responsibility. This is basically a job security, which is introduced to a person when they are being hired. HRM helps to fulfill the commitment policy by making sure that all the levels of staffing are steady. The staffing levels are set consistent with the needs of the business. The organization will also show its commitment to the employees, and it will invest in their prosperity by offering training opportunities. The organization also offers performance evaluation as well as activities for goal setting.

2. Competence

This is a value that supports the development of a business. This is also an aspect that is in the job satisfaction of the employee. It also looks at how the organization will affect the society as a whole. Majority of businesses depend on workers who are competent, and they comprehend the performance expectation of their employers. HRM will maintain the competency of the workforce by offering orientation and training. Through these, the employees will be more upgraded, and well nurtured and their skills and knowledge of the job will also be improved.

3. Cost Effectiveness

The HRM department usually has insufficient funds that will take care of all the needed activities of Human Resources. This is more so in the departments of training, recruitments, employee relations and development. One drawback of the HRM department is that it doesn't generate revenue. That is why the department will mostly be short of money. Nevertheless, this department is normally responsible for the illustration of investment returns. As a result of the investment returns, the business would benefit from high-quality services of the employees. Also, there would be efficiency, which would benefit the business greatly.

4. Congruence

The workforce management that is achievable should be congruent with all the business goals. The goals like becoming a leader of an industry should go along with the HRM hiring talented employees. The employees should be able to research and develop the company's product innovatively. The effect of congruence in the society is a business owner who offers several career opportunities. The employers provide job opportunities in the labor market that surrounds the business. Also, the employer offers the customers top notch products.

Functions Of HRM

Other than the values that guides the management of human resources, the HRM has a number of responsibilities, which include the following:

• Hiring And Training

This is among the most common responsibilities of HRM. The managers of human resources will establish plans and other strategies that help in hiring anyone who is right for the job offered. The management will design the standards that are the most ideal for the job that is offered. They also formulate the employee's duties, and the task scope that is assigned to them. They can also provide training to the recruited workers, when there is need. The employees will have the opportunity to enhance their skills, which helps them acquire more roles in the future.

• *Performance Assessments*

The HRM will also encourage the employees to work in accordance with their ability. The management of HR will also offer the employees suggestions, which helps them to enhance in their department. The employees will communicate with the staff personally and frequently. The HRM will also provide the organization with the right information regarding the performance of the employees. The management will also define the role of the employees. This helps the workers to know about their progress, and clearly understand their given roles. The appraisal of performance is mostly aimed at motivating the employees by providing them with the outline of their progress.

• *Sustaining The Atmosphere Of The Work*

The work atmosphere is very important in HRM. The employee's performance will be greatly affected by the work culture or atmosphere. There needs to be a good working condition for the sake of encouraging productivity. The environment needs to be clean, safe, comfortable, and all the necessary requirements must be considered.

• *Solving the Disputes*

It is normal for an organization to have issues, which could end up causing disputes. The dispute would rise between the employers and the employees. They would also arise among the employees themselves. The HRM will act as the neutral party, which would listen to the complaints of the two sides. The human resource management will then make sure that the dispute has been solved fairly, and the environment is peaceful.

Conclusion

The human resource management is basically responsible for the employees in the organization. The HRM will defend, discipline, and guide the employees. It is an entity that has been set up for the sake of ensuring that the human labor is provided as expected. Also, it helps to ensure the employees are provided for with the right resources for the role that they are assigned.

UNIT 2
SELECTING EMPLOYEES

Selecting employees can be a time-consuming and repetitive affair as companies are constantly looking for new employees to fill vacant posts left behind by other staff or during the expansion of a company. This one of the most crucial processes in an organization, which is why an entire department called Human resources is dedicated to doing it. Choosing the right individual to perform a particular job is very challenging. This is because the right person can bring fresh ideas and talent into the business, but the wrong one can cost the company very dearly. Seven stages make up the employee selection process. They are:

Notification

When a vacant post needs to be filled, the section in question must notify the Human Resource department of the availability of the post. The Department manager then sets out the qualifications that the job candidate needs to have, such as the minimum level of education and the number of years of relevant experience. The Human Resource department then draws up an advertisement and uses mass media to display it. In some cases, the human resource department will recruit potential candidates from certain areas or institutions such as universities and offer them a chance to go through the application or recruitment process, but that is if they meet the minimum qualifications.

Reviewing

This is the process of matching the applicant's qualifications to the job requirements. The Human Resource department may go through hundreds or even thousands of responses to the ads they put up, but the manager will only choose around a dozen people who will go to the next stage. This is known as short listing. Reviewing can be a complicated process because of the harsh economic times. In fact, some candidates may fail to go to the next stage because they are overqualified for the job at hand. On the flipside, during times of economic boom, the company may fail to find enough qualified candidates for the vacant posts available. Despite all this, the number of applicants that proceed to the next stage is usually dependent on how many candidates the company wants to interview.

Screening

Screening and Interviewing can take place simultaneously, or screening can take place before the interview. A telephone interview is the most common way of doing the screening process and is crucial for job candidates living out of the town where the interview will take place. Screening also helps to further reduce the number of candidates that will attend the interview. Managers can determine whether the candidate's job qualifications are enough to warrant him or her to attend the interview if they happen to come out of town or out of state.

Interviewing

An interview is the most familiar recruitment process to most job seekers. For an interview to be successful, the interviewer has to follow some procedures. These procedures include:

Explaining the interview structure; this is to familiarize the candidates with the processes that will take place during the interview and how much time each candidate will have with the interviewers.

Put the candidates at ease; interviews come with a lot of tension and stress. It is therefore good for the recruiters to try to relax the candidates by greeting them and make them feel at ease.

Tell the candidate about the job; a brief summary of what the job entails will help the candidates to provide responses that are within the scope of the job description.

Build up on Questions; to put the candidates at ease. The interviewer can begin by asking a series of low key but relevant questions then go on to the main questions.

Listen and analyze their answers; Listening is an important aspect of the interview both to the candidates and to the interviewer. Attentiveness is a valuable character trait for any candidate to have as it means that they will have fewer problems with listening and understanding instructions in the workplace. For the interviewer, listening helps them to analyze the candidate from a first-hand perspective using the answers they provide. Some candidates often make a superb impression from the replies they give which show they know their worth to the company.

Allow candidates to ask questions; an applicant who does not ask any questions should raise a red flag since it shows lack of interest in the company and the candidate just wants a job for the salary and benefits rather than to nurture their own talents. The type of questions asked by the applicant help the interviewer to know the character of the candidate.

Selection

After the interview, the hiring manager will ask for feedback from the human resources manager on the results of the interview. He or she may review the interview notes and select the candidate they feel will be the most productive based on the data obtained from the interview. After the hiring manager or human resource department has chosen their preferred candidate, the selected candidate will receive a notification stating that they have filled the job position. Out of courtesy, the human resource department must contact those who did not pass the interview so that they can go on and look for other opportunities elsewhere.

Testing

Candidates may go through this procedure before or after being hired. Legal procedures and company policies usually demand that a candidate must pass a drug test. Some companies also require a full medical checkup especially when taking out employee-sponsored health insurance. In the insurance industry, candidates may undergo a psychological test to determine whether they are well-suited for the job.

Induction and Training

It is the final but nonetheless important part of the employee selection process. It is at this stage that the recruiters get to see whether the candidate selected was the best fit for the company. The process entails introducing the employee to their new working environment and familiarizing them with the corporate culture of the company. The recruiters are able to monitor how quickly the employee is able to integrate him or herself into the workplace and become a productive member. Induction and training helps to reduce staff turnover and reduces the cost of selecting another employee to fill the vacant position.

UNIT 3
WORK COMPENSATION

The concept of human resource management has been developed somewhere in the 20th century, as more and more companies started to grow and need more employees. At the start-up of a business, there were not many people who thought about the employees as a useful person but rather as a person meant to deliver a service. As there was the obvious need to maximize the performance of the employee at the work place, a few smart persons have come up with the concept of human resource management. The concept worked and, throughout time, it developed to the point where it is today.

When we say human resources, we know that this a highly generous field, regarding the performance of the employee at the workplace. The employer is clearly interested in how much performance the employee delivers but he/she is also interested in the quality promised. Only by having hard-working employees, will the employer be able to reach his/her strategic objectives. The idea behind human resource management is to handle the relationship between employee and employer, among other things. Basically, it represents the sets of measures being taken for the management of the employees within the said organization.

The HR department is also responsible for the recruitment of the employees who are going to work in the company. After a person is hired, someone from the HR department is going to handle the training process of the said employee as well. Perhaps one of the most important aspects in which human resources are involved is the one of rewarding. This does not include solely the monthly paycheck given to the employee; it also refers to the other benefits that the company might offer, including annual bonuses, paid trips or other covered expenses.

Employees are compensated through human resources with the regular payroll but, as it was previously mentioned, they have a wide range of other benefits included on their contract. For example, let's say you are working in a multi-national company and your contract includes, apart from the paycheck, a wide range of benefits. The company handles your travel expenses and also delivers an annual bonus. All of these benefits are handled by the human resources department, so that the employee is satisfied. The employer takes advantage of the human resource management and makes sure that his company runs smoothly. In essence, everyone is satisfied.

How did companies realize that it was essential to introduce the concept of human resources? The answer is simple. The first businesses that developed in the 20th centuries had workers. They represented the modern equivalent of today's employees and they needed to be satisfied as well, in order to maintain the functionality of the business to the required level. As the concept of business developed, so did the one of human resources. Employees realized that they had rights and they wanted their work to be properly compensated. Suddenly, it wasn't enough to receive their paycheck. They wanted benefits. They wanted healthcare and paid travel expenses.

The human resource management concept supported the idea that the employee should receive everything he/she wanted, within normal limits. The idea behind that was that a satisfied employee is also one who is dedicated to his work. If the benefits offered appealed to the employee, that meant a reduced chance of him leaving his job for a similar position in another company. This is the major factor affecting the functionality of a company; if the human resources department does not manage to properly compensate the employees, then they will not waste their time and go to another company in an instant.

Each employee has different levels to go through, in order to advance in a company. The paycheck increases accordingly to each one of these steps and so do the benefits offered along the line. It goes without saying that the benefits offered for an entry-level job are going to be quite different from the ones offered for more advanced or experienced positions. It is the job of the human resources department to improve the economic efficiency of the company and to establish the kind of benefits offered for each work level. The pay hierarchy is essential so as to maintain order in the company.

In plain words, the best way to describe the idea of human resources is as a buffer between employer and employee. It is the bond that keeps everyone satisfied with their place of work and it helps the employer to reach targeted objectives, through its hard working employees. Major corporations have managed to defeat existing competition by relying on their human resource departments and the chosen strategies for employee compensation. By knowing how to properly compensate their employees, they have prevented them leaving the job for a similar position in a concurrent company.

The concept of human resource management is under constant evolvement, as companies continue to develop and change at the same time. Employees change, they want more from their work place and they are more than interested in the way the company values them. On the other hand, employers from major corporations have learned that employees are not just assets. They know that the satisfaction of the employee is just as valuable and rewarding as the one of the customer. And they are willing to pay for that satisfaction.

The employee has a lot to gain from the development of the human resources concept. For the first time in many years, compensation is not just about financial pay. Sure, the money is important but so are the hours offered as free time, the paid expenses guaranteed for increased functionality or the annual bonus offered to a dedicated employee. Each company might decide on the best way to compensate its employees but in the end, it all goes down to one thing: satisfaction. And satisfaction can only be obtained only through professional and modern human resource management.

UNIT 4
LAWS & POLICIES

To help uphold human rights in the workplace, it's highly important that every employer enact laws and policies that will protect the employees against any form of discrimination. Basically, these are designed with the sole purpose of ensuring that everyone, irrespective of their beliefs, is treated equally. Thus, through the enactment of these laws and policies, there's a guarantee that the workplace will be an environment that is both welcoming and respectful of all kinds of diversity. Examples of these laws and policies include, but are not limited to:

THE CODE OF CONDUCT:

A code of conduct acts as a foundation in regards to the physical or behavioral standards under which the employees have to carry themselves. These codes are fundamentally influenced by the type of organization. Some of the areas covered under this policy include the dress code (how the employees are supposed to dress - like whether they should wear uniforms, or day(s) of the week when they should wear uniforms, or if they should dress in smart casual or business dresses). To meet the needs of both the employer and the employee, the two should sit down and discuss on what's appropriate and what's not. Also, every new employee should have the dress requirements outlined carefully in their appointment letters.

Under the code of conduct, there also should be a sub-policy detailing how and when the employees should use the internet, the social media and their company emails. While an employee shouldn't use them inappropriately, like using the internet to visit pornographic websites, s/he should also be given privacy so that they don't feel as though their internet communications are always under Big Brother's watch.

DISCIPLINARY POLICY AND TERMINATION POLICY (PROTECTION AGAINST RETALIATION):

In essence, the termination policy is set to protect employees against any form of wrongful termination, especially if the termination is as a result of them taking legal action against the organization laws and/or policies, or by simply airing their grievances on the same. The best way of enacting this policy is by having the human resource managers create a documentation process that has to be followed every time an employee has to be fired. That way, an employee cannot sue for illegal termination.

On the other hand, the disciplinary policy should outline the appropriate action that should be taken against an employee after failing to perform their duties or adhere to the company laws and policies. Though the action taken is meant to correct the behavior of the employee, it shouldn't be so harsh that it gets in the way of their human rights or performance.

SAFETY IN THE WORKPLACE:

Under the Organizational Health & Safety Act

(OSHA), an employee is entitled to a safe workplace failure to which they can refuse to work. Thus, if an employee is injured while working under an unsafe work environment, they are free to sue for compensation. The same applies if the company fails to address viable injuries from around the workplace, such as robberies and assaults that employees may face while going to or coming from work.

ANTI-DISCRIMINATORY POLICY - EMPLOYMENT AND RECRUITMENT EQUITY:

Essentially, this is set to ensure that all people, but most specifically the minority groups, are given equal opportunities in the workplace. These include women, people with disabilities, individuals from minority groups and the Aboriginal people.

This policy has to be exercised when a job vacancy is being advertised, during the recruitment process and also, after employment. Therefore, every company is expected to offer everyone, irrespective of their nationality, religious beliefs, marital status, gender, disability, ethnicity, sexual orientation or age the same opportunities before or while working for/with them.

ANTI-HARASSMENT POLICY - PROTECTION AGAINST SEXUAL HARASSMENT:

Since sexual harassment being one of the most common forms of harassment in the workplace, it's important that everyone be trained on what is or may be considered sexual harassment. All employees should also be given the right to take part in airing any complaints or concerns that they may help in keeping the workplace safe for all. Above all this, the employer should adhere to these policies so as to lead by example.

It's worth noting that sexual harassment is not only limited to women, but to men as well.

LEAVE POLICY:

Due to the variance on the types of leaves available, there has to be a policy that outlines how each of these leaves has to be managed. The best way of doing this is by having the employer give an outline of the types of leaves available, how the employees ought to go about applying for one, who should give the approval, duration of the leave, whether the leave is paid or unpaid and other terms and conditions surrounding the leave.

In a nutshell, workplace laws and policies should always set out the intended purpose of the given policy, give a thorough explanation of what may have led to the development of that policy, give a detailed list of the persons whom the policy applies, set out what is considered acceptable or unacceptable, indicate the consequences that are bound to come by if one fails to comply with the policy and, give a date of when the policy was first developed and when it was last updated.

IMPORTANCE OF ENACTING WORKPLACE LAWS AND POLICIES:

They help in clarifying the responsibilities and functions of both the employees and the employer. Gives proof that the organization is being run efficiently and effectively. Ensures that the organization complies with the employment legislation. Comes in handy when the company's performance and accountability is being assessed. Saves on times. This is based on the fact that these laws and policies act as a guide when a problem needs to be addressed. The employee's strength is given a boost especially when dealing with legal matters. They foster continuity and stability for the company.

Since these laws and policies are designed to cater for the needs of the employer and the employee, both parties should be involved in forming and implementing them. This is because doing so makes it easier for everyone to work towards creating a respectful workplace for not just themselves, but others as well.

The myriad of federal and state laws that govern the place of work are vast and complex. Complying with these legalities is crucial to running a business. Numerous aspects of business are regulated by the federal regulations including the labor, business and employment laws which are amongst the most carefully checked. While the larger businesses can hire HRs and attorney to ensure that the business is always up to date with the most recent of laws, those who own smaller businesses may find that they have a huge problem when it comes to knowing what is up to date. Some even think that they can "fly under the radar" when it comes to the much bigger labor laws. There are things small business owners should know so that they are always at the right side of the law every time.

1. The national labor relations act (NLRA)

> If you are a business owner, you should not assume that the laws of the NLRA do not apply to you just because none of your employees are in any union. The law usually protects far more employees than just those who are in the union. The NLRA applies, with a few exceptions to all private employers who are engaged in interstate commerce. It is a

way of guaranteeing that all employees are given their rights and can be organized and bargain with the employers accordingly.

2. The Americans with disability Act (ADA)

In all employment practices, which include the job application procedure, hiring, firing, privileges accorded to employees and training among others, ADA ensures that there is no discrimination amongst the "qualified individuals with disabilities". Disability is a word that is very important and each employer should know what it is they are expected to do. A person with disability according to the law is one who:

- Has a mental or physical impairment that limits to a great extent one or more major life activities

- Has a record of limiting impairments

- Is regarded as having such impairments.

People who do not have conditions that limit major life activity are not considered disabled. It is therefore important that you learn how to determine if a worker is covered by the law or not.

3. Family and medical leave act (FMLA)

This is the most complex and most confused of all the laws that govern the workplace. Generally, as an employer your are required to grant any eligible employee 12 work weeks of unpaid leave during any 12 month period for either one or more of the following reasons:

- The birth and care of a newborn of the employee

- For caring for an immediate family member with a serious condition

- Medical leave when the employee is not able to work for serious health reasons

- When the employee is placed with a son or daughter for adoption

It may be difficult to recognize an employee with FMLA unless they are clearly pregnant. As an employer you are therefore burdened with the task of verifying and getting all the medical facts right about any employee requesting medical leave.

UNIT 5
STAFF TRAINING & MOTIVATION

A properly trained workforce is a company's most prized asset. When employees go through appropriate training, they realize their involvement and importance in the company in a much better way. Consequently they become motivated and loyal to the company not because they lack other choices but because they understand their importance and responsibilities. Thus a good staff training program must develop focusing on the following traits:

- Understanding

- Improvement

- Career Opportunities

- Continuous

- Valued Employees

Understanding: Regardless of department or workload, each employee participates in a company's advancement. However, the problem is a large portion of the staff often fails to see how they are doing it and thus remain only mildly motivated. Training programs help employees to understand how their jobs are contributing to the whole system and how they are not just another clog in the wheel. Understanding responsibilities is vital for individual development.

Improvement: Most employees unintentionally become specialized on a specific type of job and their understanding often exceeds that of a supervising individual (like a manager). Unfortunately they also often lack the proper educational training and tools to put these enhanced knowledge to us. A good staff training program must always be able to fulfill these intellectual and materialistic needs.

Career Opportunities: When an individual joins a company's staff force, they come in expecting the current post as a starting position, not the final one. When that company fails to offer the expected training and opportunities to employees, they become uninterested and unmotivated towards the company's ultimate objective. Gradually lethargy sets into the whole force. Every step of a staff training program must focus on teaching something new and thus making individuals more versatile towards new roles and opportunities.

Continuous: A company goes through changes from the beginning to the end. Thus, employees also need to be trained from the day they join the company to the day they retire or cease to be a part of the staff. Otherwise some would fall back while others prosper creating imbalance in the force.

Valued Employees: When a company offers training programs for its employees, it sends out a message that it appreciates what they do. This also indicates that the company values progress not for progress's sake only but because it also creates opportunities for the contributing individuals. When a program manages to send out this message, employees become more psychologically attached to the organization seeing it not as a separate entity but as a collection of responsible individuals.

Often small organizations say that they cannot afford training programs for their employees or they just do not have the time. Problem is, regardless of company size, an untrained or under-trained staff is incapable of using its fullest potential and consequently the company keeps losing a steady flow of profits. A training program does not need to be expensive to be effective; it just needs to be properly organized. Let us take a look at the steps through which a staff force can be trained regardless of new or old employees.

1. Delegate the training responsibilities to people with the proper experience and willingness. Selecting instructors because they are simply in the closest proximity of the individual(s) and have the most amount of expendable time is a recipe for disaster.

2. In case of a new hire, training should not just focus on teaching the professional responsibilities but also socializing them into the organization's informal environment. This should drastically enhance the hire's learning capacity.

3. The goal and steps of a training program should be put in written form and shared with all the participants. Literal visualization helps people in staying focused and motivates them since they know where all this is going.

4. A good training program requires a safe environment for learning. If an individual(s) feels uncertain about their progress, they start feeling isolated and unwanted. It is a

trainer's responsibility to make sure nothing like this happens by treating the trainee as a human being with feelings, not just another objective to be fulfilled. Trainees should be able to realize that it takes time to learn something new or upgrade an existing skill.

5. The training pace should be decided in a participative manner. This means trainees should also be consulted in deciding how fast the program should be carried on. This is especially important when there are multiple trainers since their schedules might turn out to be too overlapping leaving not enough room for sustaining new lessons.

6. When training new employees or old employees for new roles, providing them with a detailed manual of their new jobs and responsibilities is a great idea. This way they would not be confused thinking whether something is expected of them or not.

7. Eliminate negativity from the program. Both trainers and trainees should remember that if something has been done before, it can be done again. Negativity is a common problem when new technology is introduced to older employees. Both parties must keep in mind that not everyone learns at the same speed, some have to work harder than others. Replacing negative sentences like "I don't think I can do this" with "I'll try to the best of my ability" is also a good idea.

8. Avoid cross-training. Remember that training is for teaching something new and people cannot learn too many new

things simultaneously, especially when the different ideas do not complement each other. Otherwise all the new introductions will suffer.

9. Feedback is the best catalyst a training program can provide for its participants. If detailed feedback is provided after each session or segment, employees will know exactly how much they have improved from the previous period. Employees can develop a sense of achievement this way and manage to stay motivated for longer.

10. Lastly, be generous with positive comments. Providing employees with playful yet constructive criticism is a lot better than coming down hard on them. In fact, studies show that it is counter-productive and gradually reduces an employee's efficiency.

A good training program does not try to change an employee's personal traits but adds new skills to the existing set. Micromanaging is the best way to confuse a trainee's personal attributes which in no way helpful of the program. A participant must be considered as someone who already has enough capacity to learn what the program wishes to teach.

UNIT 6
STAFF DEVELOPMENT

Staff development is defined as the programs and activities (informal or formal and off or on the organization) that help staff members develop required competencies and skills and learn about responsibilities that are necessary to accomplish institutional and divisional purposes and goals, and grow professionally and personally in order to prepare themselves for advancement in the organization or beyond. Because individual goals, job descriptions, and even an institution's mission, department, or division may change, staff development plans ought to be reviewed on a regular basis and changes to the staff development plan made as and when necessary- with both the supervisor and staff members being in agreement on the intended changes.

A staff development plan should thus be formulated with the following objectives in mind:

1. Specify available options for staff improvement

2. Clarify expectations for the progressive education of staff members

3. Ensure adequate funding for development activities aimed at improving staff

4. Establish a clear connection between institutional rewards and continuous professional development.

5. Employ accepted methods of learning and teaching in staff development activities.

6. Purposefully determine staff development activities in accordance with the needs of each staff member.

Use of the staffing model in developing staff

The integrated staffing module postulates a close relationship between performance appraisal and staff development. This is because like the former, staff development practices are dependent upon the context of the organization. It thus follows that an effective staff development model ought to be congruent with:

1. Goals and mission of the organization

2. Goals and mission of individual departments

3. Job description for the position that each staff member occupies

4. The appropriate professional association's professional practice statement

5. The goals of each individual staff member.

Comprehensive and effective staff development practices must, therefore, attend to organizational and staff improvement, include attention to both product and process, derive from a developmental plan, be ever changing and multi-faceted, be anchored in day-to-day work, and recognize growth and maturation in staff. This is further explained below as follows:

Development Plan

Staff development ought to be active, intentional, and potent. Individual growth plans should be a reflection of current professional and personal status regarding attributes that are needed to perform assigned tasks, long- and short-term goals, and alternative ways of achieving those goals. Additionally, there should be a plan for organizational improvement, with both the organization's and individual's needs addressed in this plan.

Dual purposes: Organization and Staff Development

Staff development practices are characterized by a dual focus in that they must attend to not only organizational development, but individual staff development as well. For staff development to be considered a success, both goals have to be met i.e. they must mutually support each other. Such a commitment requires flexibility and creativity in staff development plans.

Anchored in Day-to-Day Activities

Since staff development is an ongoing process, it should be anchored in day-to-day work thus making it visible in all personnel functions in the division/department. Similarly, all other staffing functions should be related to staff development- especially in performance appraisal and supervision.

Product and Process

The objective of staff development is to improve organizational effectiveness together with staff. It is thus little surprise that this process affects relationships with colleagues, interpretations of job requirements, and perspectives on educational methods. Ideally, staff development should occur in a social context and emphasize teamwork, founded on collaboration. It should demonstrate the commonness of purpose by staff in addition to the crucial nature of individual skills and knowledge necessary to carry out assigned duties geared towards the achievement of larger goals.

Recognizes Growth and Maturation

The staff development process must be cognizant of the variations in the growth and maturity of the organization and individuals. While some staff members may have served for years, others could be in the initial stages of their professional careers. Also, the roles of staff members may change in time with those affected requiring retooling in order to better adapt to their new responsibilities.

Ever-Changing and Multifaceted

With staff development being targeted at different people in different roles, it must continuously evolve. Staff development activities should thus require thoughtful reflection and integration couched in the context of what each particular job entails. This is likely to lead to desired effects on staff behavior as well.

Components Involved in Training Staff Professionally

These include:

1. Selection, Recruitment, and Retention

These are defined as all the activities associated with identifying potential staff members, identifying those who best fit the organization and job, and providing requisite systems and activities geared toward ensuring that they stay for as long as possible.

2. Performance coaching

Administrators and staff members should work together to develop performance plans and engage continuously in leading and motivating members. Effective coaching paves the way for staff members to foster stronger relationships besides working collaboratively to attain organizational goals.

3. Assessing Performance

Performance appraisals are vital in establishing and maintaining conditions necessary for effective performance management. When facilitated properly, they among others confirm that staff members understand their roles, evaluate the extent to which performance goals are being met, identify barriers and problems in the workplace, provide constructive and positive feedback, encourage regular work-related conversations between staff members and supervisors, and provide information that provides the basis for the performance reward process.

4. Rewarding Performance

Compensation aligned with organizational goals is a sure way to facilitate development. The performance reward process entails the allocation of a staff member's salary together with their benefits. And when effectively implemented, it provides a platform for specific consequences for feedback and actual performance regarding the merit of accomplishments.

5. Staff Development

Staff development refers to all the activities that directly or indirectly affect the ability of a staff member to do their current or future job. This entails identifying competencies needed by staff and ensuring that any development is geared toward enhancing such competencies. This could take the form of on-the-job training, professional conferences, on-site programs and workshops, and new employee orientation.

6. Planning and Developing Careers

Planning careers consists of the systematic approach that ensures each staff member's skills, values, and interests meet the organization's needs and requirements. Conversely, career development may consist of career planning workshops, tuition reimbursement, career coaching, staff orientation programs, job enrichment, and release time to pursue graduate classes.

7. Transition

Needless to say, some staff members may leave the organization, either involuntarily or voluntarily. Whatever the case, it is vital that supervisors make such transitions as seamless as possible by ensuring that those who leave are equipped with the necessary knowledge and skills to transition into their next position.

UNIT 7
TERMINATION

Terminating an employee without following the right procedure and creating a plan of action can lead to lawsuits since it is illegal for the firing to be a surprise. However, this article will exclusively explore the right procedure for legally terminating an employee.

Preparing to terminate an employee is very important since it ensures that the laws are not violated. Also, it is important to ensure that the human resources attorney is consulted before taking any step to fire an employee in order to ensure the bases are covered.

It is advisable to think through and review the decision for termination since it may be due to the heat of anger. However, taking some time to reflect and having careful review of all relevant documents and facts helps to come up with a good decision.

Holding a carefully planned termination meeting is very crucial since it reduces emotional distress to the employee being discharged. Also, this meeting minimizes potential legal liability and protects the employees and property of the company.

The employee should be treated with respect and dignity in the termination meeting by ensuring that there is follow up after firing. However, the discharged employee can be shown sensitivity to the employee's reaction and being allowed to speak with the other employees after the meeting.

www.ingramcontent.com/pod-product-compliance
Lightning Source LLC
Chambersburg PA
CBHW070425190526
45169CB00003B/1413